JUST BE...

Your Path to Meditation and Awareness

The mindful way to love your life

Thank you for shining your light in this world Debbie 2019

By

D J M Sodergren

Copyright © 2015 by D J M Sodergren

www.debbiesodergren.com

Published by Infinite Joy Publishing

PO Box 57973, Murray Utah 84157

All rights reserved. No part of this book may be reproduced in any form without permission in writing from the author. Reviewers may quote brief passages in reviews.

Disclaimer

No part of this publication may be reproduced or transmitted in any form or by any means, mechanical or electronic, including photocopying or recording, or by any information storage and retrieval system, or transmitted by email without permission in writing from the publisher.

While all attempts and efforts have been made to verify the information held within this publication, neither the author nor the publisher assumes any responsibility for errors, omissions, or opposing interpretations of the content herein.

This book is for entertainment purposes only. The views expressed are those of the author alone, and should not be taken as expert instruction or commands. The reader of this book is responsible for his or her own actions when it comes to reading the book.

Adherence to all applicable laws and regulations, including international, federal, state, and local governing professional licensing, business practices, advertising, and all other aspects of doing business in the US, Canada, or any other jurisdiction is the sole responsibility of the purchaser or reader.

Neither the author nor the publisher assumes any responsibility or liability whatsoever on the behalf of the purchaser or reader of these materials.

Any received slight of any individual or organization is purely unintentional.

Acknowledgements

For over 15 years now I have been working and compiling this information in a way so that the people who took my class were able to get the best results. This book would not be what it is today if it wasn't for the many students over the years who gave me feedback from my classes. I want to thank those friends and family and the people I didn't know who courageously signed up and showed up to my class.

I want to thank the weekly meditation group I attended that was across the street from my home back in the 1990's. Flo and all her meditation friends welcomed me in and listened to my insights and encouraged me that someday I was going to write this book.

I want to thank all the administrators who interviewed me and allowed me to explain my class and then graciously allowed me to teach in their facility.

To the tribe of like-minded thinkers I belong to that we affectionately refer to ourselves as 'Ippies'...your support and friendships has given me the courage to not only move forward with this book but to also stand up on stage and share my insights and speak my truth from my perception. Thank you for the unconditional love and understanding and shared vision of living our authentic lives. You know who you are, I am excited and happy to be on this journey with you.

I want to thank my publisher and friend April, thank you for believing in my book and all the support. You have been a great guide in this process. Ever since we met in Boston at the IP training event, we knew we were connected and would do some amazing things together!

Dedication

For Cassie, Drew and Corey

Thank you for blessing me with being your mom. You inspire me and I am in awe of each of you. I love you more than this world, bigger than the universe.

For Shawn

Thank you for loving me unconditionally. I know I challenged you with some of my thinking and my interest in metaphysical studies and you honored me by supporting me. You are patient, kind, trusting, supportive and you have always done your best so I feel equal in our relationship. I am honored to be sharing my life with you. (3 squeezes of our hands ☺)

Introduction

Everyone has their "stuff" they go through. We all experience what we perceive as challenges or difficult things to persevere through. These experiences make us who we are. They do not define us, but rather they integrate into who we are evolving into as spiritual beings having a human experience. This is my experience of my own challenges. I share this with you, the reader so you have a better understanding of what I have been through and how it has shaped me into knowing all I share in my writing.

I grew up with both parents, siblings and had the blessing of my aunts, uncles, cousins, grandparents and great grandmother – I refer to this as a tribal upbringing, I was raised by all of them. It's a rare thing to experience and we are all still very close today.

When I was 4 years old, I had open heart surgery twice to repair a hole in my heart. Everyone is born with a hole in their heart and it closes up on its own by the age of four. While getting my kindergarten physical, my doctor noticed my hole hadn't closed. I was seen by a specialist who recommended I have open heart surgery.

After my 1st surgery, my parents came into my room to see me. My mom noticed that my color was 'funny' and said so to the surgeon. My parents were asked to step outside my room while I was evaluated. While sitting outside my room waiting to see me, staff members were bringing in units of blood for me because I was bleeding out internally. After evaluating me, the surgeon told my parents that he needed to go in again and repair the hole since the stitches he put in were not holding the tissue together. Apparently, while I was being moved from the surgery table to a gurney the stitches tore.

I had the 2nd surgery and all went well. I'm not sure which surgery it happened during, but during one of my surgeries, I had an out of body experience. I remember it but when I try to explain it, it's my 4 year old self that explains it. Let me show you: I remember floating above my body and slowly looking down at the body of 'her' on the table and the doctor and nurses around her. I remember this spaghetti string of gold light going from my belly button to hers. I remember turning back upward and continuing to go up, up, up. It was bright with white light yet I would feel these soap bubbles pass by me and when we connected, it was like I knew everything there was to know about that soap bubble as if they were a person. I felt happy, giddy happy. I was not afraid. I felt loved and safe and so connected to everything around me. I remember realizing that I needed to go back to 'her' because I had a family and friends that I wanted to see again. I felt I would return to this place someday and I wasn't sad to leave it.

In the next few days, I was instructed that I could ride a tricycle around the hospital floor and stop at the elevator and press the button to stretch my scar.

My scar is cut like a smiley face on the right side of my body underneath my breast. My doctor cut me that way because I am a girl and he didn't want me to have the big scar down the middle of my chest. I thank him to this day for that foresight, Thank you again Dr. Coffin. I healed. I have never been medicated for dental procedures, I had three beautiful babies naturally and a cardiologist was on call, "just in case" and "just in case" never happened.

After I returned home from my surgery, I had these vivid "dreams" of leaving my body and visiting my grandparents sleeping across the street in their house or visiting my best friend who lived next door. I didn't think much of it, and thought everyone could do it.

I remember sharing this information with an adult who told me not talk about it because it wasn't 'normal' and people would not understand and may think I was weird or be afraid of me. So, I forced myself to stop doing it. When I would go to sleep at night, I would begin to experience the feeling of leaving my body, and I would force myself to not do it, and as a result, I stopped doing it altogether.

It wasn't until I turned 18 that something shifted inside of me. I had a traumatic experience. Maybe it was anger from what happened, maybe it was shame or maybe it was both. I sought out a crisis counselor and I was able to release a significant amount of rage. That did help me, but then something else started to shift in me, something was calling me to look at all the events that had happened in my life so far, and evaluate the things I observed while growing up in my family. I was curious to see if this could help me get to the feeling of understanding who I truly am.

I heard about a workshop in New York City called 'Women, Sex & Power' and decided I needed to attend it. I borrowed money from relatives, figured out the train to New York, found someone to share a room with and attended the workshop. It was a really great experience and I felt like I was beginning the healing process. In the workshop, I was encouraged to share my painful experience and I was led through steps to release the pain. Now remember, this was done in a large group setting and it was very comforting because everyone in the room was releasing their own painful experience simultaneously. There was something magical about doing this in a large group, almost as if the energy was magnified and the healing had a deeper magnitude. It felt awesome.

Later that year, I also consulted a psychic who made predictions about my life to come, all of which came true. She told me about where I was going to live, how many kids I was going to have, and other information and she was right. During this time, I started to remember my out of body experience that happened (I think) during my second open heart surgery. It wasn't until after the birth of my daughter that I was able to recall all the details in its entirety.

I've heard somewhere when people go through a stressful or traumatic event, their world suddenly changes and they are able to experience a sudden in -depth awareness. I didn't start piecing these things together until I was turning 30.

I had a recurring dreadful feeling my husband was going to die and I was only going to have ten years of our life together. I shared this anxiety with one of my aunts who suggested I go see a friend of hers. Her friend explained to me that I was opening to my psychic abilities and I was remembering my past lives, and as a result the wires of this life, and past were being crossed. She explained the concept of free will and inquired as to what exactly I was going to do about it, moreover what was I going to change? So, I made the conscious decision to see myself living a long healthy life with my husband, many years into our marriage, enjoying children and grandchildren. She suggested I continue to take classes in metaphysical subjects and work on the new path my life was presenting to me. I am happy to say, my husband and I have been together for over 25 years now.

For me, all of these experiences were helping me to remember who I AUTHENTICALLY am. They were showing me that all the things I experienced in my life – were there by divine design – by the choices I made. Now, I know this might be hard for everyone to comprehend because it essentially means that we need to take full responsibility for what we experience in our lives.

Remember when I said earlier I experienced something traumatic at the age of 18? Through training and studying different metaphysical and parapsychology subjects, I can now view that experience from a third person perspective, removing my emotional attachment and as a result I can see that my action of going into a boy's room alone was my choice. Was it my choice that he acted the way he did and hurt me? No, however what I have learned is it wasn't my fault, I am not responsible for his actions, but it DID happen. I now know and understand that because of that experience, I now make the kinds of choices that keep me safe, and to share that experience with others so they may learn from it. I am not a victim, it doesn't define me, and instead it is just an experience that shaped me into who I am evolving into today. Without that experience, I would not have made the choices throughout my life that got me to become the person I am today. My conscious choices, became my thoughts, which became real in my life. Now, as I continue on my journey of living my life by my own design, I can see it more clearly. I am able to connect the dots. I can see now that as I think of something terrible in my life, it is simply my perception of that experience, if I sit with it long enough – hold onto it with grace and quietness – I am able to see the value in it. The gift it has brought me.

Again, this is my perception. I know all things are connected – a spark of divine intelligence from what I call Source– we are really wonderful spiritual beings having a human experience. I understand that my brain is the computer by which my bodily systems are run automatically. But, our minds shape our perception and our heart is the epicenter of our emotions, which impacts our mind and shapes our perception. I know we are not the most intelligent life forms. I know these as truths and it doesn't bother me that science cannot prove it... yet. I

KNOW, in my gut, where intuition resides that someday they will.

There were civilizations who existed before us – they relied solely upon the heavens and stars to guide them – I also choose to allow that guidance to be my navigator. So I will continue to live my life as my authentic self and harness the brilliance of those who have mastered their gift to fulfill their purpose here and I choose to do this dance called life with them. I will continue to connect with the knowledge I am getting from my spirit and embrace the knowledge that is returning to me, spark by spark. So, with this said, I invite you, the reader to open your mind and your heart to the possibility of using new tools to solve old patterns and to live in joy and less struggle.

I love the following quote from Henry Ford:

"If you think you can or you think you can't, you are right."

Table of Contents

Week 1:

INTRODUCTION TO

MEDITATION AND AWARENESS

Quiet the mind, and the soul will speak.

—MA JAYA SATI BHAGAVATI

I have come to learn over time that people have difficulty learning meditation. This 4 week course is designed to orient the potential student in the practice of creating a life they love using meditation to achieve the valuable benefits of health, stress reduction and living a life with mindfulness. This course will cover understanding meditation, the origins of meditation and how to heal your body and mind with meditation. It will also touch on the different mental disciplines used in meditation from

Christian to Eastern mantras. You will learn how meditation promotes relaxation by obtaining balance from the mind, body and spirit. Meditation has been used for centuries as a tool to not only alter consciousness but to alleviate physical and mental distress.

I began teaching this information in this specific order laid out here in this book, back in 1998 after I moved to Minnesota. One night after putting the kids to bed, I sat up all night and this information, manifested into what I called a course that I would teach. I have since taught this information to hundreds of people through the years and whether they were an experienced meditator or new to meditation, everyone felt they shifted in their experience in taking my course for 4 weeks. Recently, I decided with the encouragement of a few students and friends, to write this book so more people could benefit from how I taught meditation. There are a few important things to know before you begin. It is helpful if you wear comfortable loose non-constricting clothing, the use of a meditation pillow you can sit on or lie down on the floor is beneficial. It is also very important to drink plenty of water and stay hydrated for these next four weeks, you are shifting energy and you need to flush water through your body's system. I also strongly encourage you to take notes.

Writing about your experiences with meditation is REALLY important, so get a journal. In addition, exercises will be provided in this book and keeping them in the journal would be ideal to refer back to so you are able to see your growth in your perspective.

I have written this book for you to follow and practice what you learn in weekly intervals. In week one we will be learning the following principles:

- Why are you wanting to learn meditation?

- What meditation is, and what it is not

- Using breath with intention

- How to set the scene to accomplish your meditation goals

- How to get comfortable

- Introduction to the Sun Salutation

- Use of the candle flame exercise

- Introduction to the concept of being a co-creator

The first thing I'd like for you to do is answer this question in the space below: Why do I want to learn to meditate? *Write this down below:*

To be more centered and focused during the day. Increase circulation / healing of my body.

Meditation is a state of mind, it is a point of view about the world and ourselves as we interact in it. It is my belief that meditation starts within our hearts. It is having unconditional love for ourselves first, then for the world around us. Meditation is a state of total awareness that is brought on by physical relaxation. It is free from self-centered emotions or personal opinions.

When we achieve this state of awareness, we are able to view the world around us from a different perspective. One in which we are looking at ourselves interacting within the world. This expanded perception and awareness awakens our senses to the larger universe at play, one in which we are part of a bigger picture.

To choose the discipline to meditate on a regular basis is allowing yourself the freedom to watch, listen and communicate with yourself. You become more open and willing to allow yourself to co-create your life. Many individuals struggle with the idea that we are co-creators of our lives. The question has been asked many times over many years is, who or what is assisting us with co-creating our lives? The partner and co-creator that we work with has many names, such as, Your Higher Self, Universal Consciousness, Source, God, The Universe, Divine Intelligence, Buddha, Allah, etc. The point is not to get caught up in what the co-creator is called, but to acknowledge that you are an integral part of the co-creation process.

I would like to cover what meditation is not. It is not hypnosis, auto suggestion, a dream state or a sleep state. It's not black magic, voodoo or Wiccan. Let's move on.

The tools and techniques you are about to learn are very simple and will help to engage you in order to achieve the state of meditation. I present them in this specific order so you receive the best results. Some of these techniques are physical activities, for example, closing your eyes, sitting in a chair, sitting with crossed legs on the floor, lying down, walking in a labyrinth, going for a run outdoors in nature, doing a sun salutation or simply focusing on your breath. There are numerous techniques that we will cover. Regardless of which of these tools or techniques you choose,

I want you to understand that there are many ways to meditate and they are all correct. I would like you to discover the best method for you right now, and have tools that will work for you later on, because the only constant is change and something that is working for you now, may not work for you down the road.

By using the above methods, we allow ourselves to relax and achieve the state of meditation, which is a state of BEING rather than DOING. In our society, we have been socially programmed to take action in order to feel like we have accomplished something. However, I would like to share with you how important it is to just BE vs. DOING. They are both equally important, unfortunately, "being" is not something we are taught to participate in on a regular basis.

When you achieve the state of meditation, science has proven that it can promote healing, improve clarity and help you experience your life's purpose.

The following are scientific facts that show the benefits of meditation for your body. It has been scientifically proven to:

- Overcome stress

- Boost your creativity

- Improve your sex life

- Increase your libido

- Cultivate healthy habits that can lead to weight loss

- Improve digestion

- Lower blood pressure

- Decrease your risk of heart attack

- Help to overcome anxiety

- Help with depression

- Help you deal with anger and confusion

- Decrease perception of pain

- Improve your cognitive processing

- Increase your focus and

- Increase the size of your most important organ— your brain!

"Meditation brings wisdom; lack of meditation leaves ignorance. Know well what leads you forward and what holds you back, and choose the path that leads to wisdom."

- Buddha

When you begin to practice meditation, you will use a type of physical activity to help you achieve the state of meditation. This is so you can receive the very best results. In addition to physical activity, there are some mental tools you will use, for example, focusing on a candle flame, following a guided visualization or focusing on an object of sentimental or spiritual value.

STEPS TO MEDITATION

STEP ONE: Setting the Scene. You are going to create an area in your home where you can go to practice meditating. This space should be located in a quiet area of your home. I recommend that you have a comfortable chair and small table where you can place a candle, have something that can play meditation music, water to drink, a photo or a special object that gives you a deep calming effect. If you are unable to have a lit candle, you can use a battery operated tea light candle. I often use these when I travel or when I teach classes where an open flame may not be allowed.

STEP TWO: Wear comfortable clothing. During meditation it is very important to be comfortable, and not wear clothing that is constrictive in any way, as it can and will break your concentration. If you meditate in the morning, do it in your pajamas. If you meditate in the evening after work, after dinner or after the kids have gone to bed, I suggest wearing either your pajamas or a comfy pair of yoga pants and a comfortable shirt. It is not important what you wear, you don't need to have a meditation outfit, but it is important as to how the clothing makes you feel. I also recommend having a zip up sweatshirt or a blanket nearby in the event you get cold. Quite often when you meditate, as your body relaxes, your body temperature can drop, leaving you feeling chilled. I encourage you to not wear shoes, but socks are appropriate.

STEP THREE: Breathing. Your breathing will be deliberate and conscious. You will begin by taking a deep breath in through your nose, hold it for two seconds and release it through your mouth with expelled force. During your inhale, allow your abdomen to expand outward. On your exhale, pull your belly button in towards your spine. When you breathe in this manner, it allows the lower chambers of your lungs to fill and you eliminate stale air that is susceptible to bacteria and can make you sick.

You will take three breaths in this manner. They are called cleansing/centering breaths. Another purpose to this deliberate breathing is to occupy your mind, not allowing thoughts to distract you from meditation. Many times we have so many things to do, we let them overrun our brains, and this kind of breathing doesn't allow you to worry about your 'to-do' list. If this still happens, here is a ***tool***; as you are sitting with your eyes closed, I want you to 'see' with your mind's eye, the 3rd eye located between your two eyebrows in the center of your forehead, see the distraction thought come in on the right side of your brain, acknowledge it by a nod of your head or a thought to yourself "I know I need to do that...ok...I see you", and allow it to go out of your head on the left side. Another ***tool*** is to imagine that the 3rd eye is a TV screen. Every time a thought pops onto the screen to distract you, turn a make believe dial and see the thought disappear like you are changing the channel. The channel you want to 'see' is of white or yellow light.

STEP FOUR: Protection. This is for you to surround yourself with beautiful white light of protection. This *tool* should encase the outside of your body like an eggshell. It can radiate about 2-3 inches around your body. When I was taught to do this, it was explained to me that it is considered a light of protection so while you are in this state of consciousness, all good things can open up to you. Your body is made of atoms that are vibrating at a range to keep all your cells together. Hence, you also have this vibrational energy which extends outward of your human body to a field around you. This field is your Auric Field. Your auric field is an amazing source of information. It actually 'feels' things that stay unnoticed until they manifest in the human body. The vibrations of your aura are always changing. Your aura reflects the general state of your *being,* including your physical, mental, emotional and spiritual health. It was taught to me and I pass this along to you, to surround yourself with this light of protection at least two times a day. The first time being right before you get up in the morning, and the second time as you lie in bed right before you go to sleep. I also use it if I am confronted by someone who is angry or a situation that makes me uncomfortable, I will mentally surround myself with the white light of protection for the purpose of protecting my energy field from any negative attachments.

Using the candle flame exercise is another ***tool***. This is an exercise I really enjoy. First you must obtain a candle or battery tea light, whichever will work for you. After you have found a comfortable place to sit, wearing appropriate clothing, and you have done your cleansing breaths, (you can also play some soft music) you will dim or turn off the lights and light your candle. You will begin by staring at the flame for about ten seconds and then close your eyes. You will then attempt to see the candle flame with your third eye which is located in the center of your forehead. It is perfectly fine and normal if you don't at first, so don't worry if you don't. With practice you will be able to. When you can no longer "see" the flame there, open your eyes again and watch the flame. Repeat this several times. Frequently, the flame you will 'see' with your third eye when your eyes are closed will be white or purple or another color, or may be just the outline of the flame. It may even move or fade out. Whatever you experience is correct. The purpose of this exercise is to give your mind something to focus on so it doesn't wander off and distract your attention away from your intention, which is to bring focus into your body, relax and gain all the benefits from meditation.

The next step is to put this all together. You can get a recording of this on my website which you can use to go through the process.

This week's exercise is called the sun salutation. This is considered a movement meditation. People who have a hard time sitting still in the beginning, like to use this **tool**. Follow this step by step guide. Remember it is important to breathe! Generally, in yoga, a rule of thumb for breathing is to breathe in on the backwards bend, and breathe out on the forward bends. Always check with your doctor before beginning any exercise.

UP VIBRATIONS

ENERGY EXPERIENCE EMPOWER

12. Salutation Position
Normal restful breathing

1. Salutation Position
Normal restful breathing

2. Raised Arms Position
Inhale

11. Raised Arms Position
Inhale

3. Hand to Foot Position
Exhale

10. Hand to Foot Position
Exhale

4. Equestrian Position
Inhale

9. Equestrian Position
Inhale

Sun Salutation

5. Mountain Position
Exhale

8. Mountain Position
Exhale

7. Cobra Position
Inhale

6. Eight Limbs Position
No breathing, then...

Each week I will give you an exercise to practice the week. It's important to do the practices I have taught you in the week before moving on. If you choose to practice and follow my instructions, you will begin to enjoy the wonderful benefits to meditation.

PRACTICE EXERCISE FOR WEEK ONE

TO DO THIS WEEK:

1. Find a place in your home that you feel is a good location that you can go and participate in the act of meditation. Find a spot to place a chair so you can sit comfortably with your feet flat on the ground and your hands on your lap. Place a table near this chair so you can place your cell phone if you use it for music and/or a timer, place a candle, drinking water, and anything else that would make this a sacred space.

2. When you have the space mentioned above all set, sit in the chair and close your eyes and do your three cleansing/centering breaths. Surround yourself with the white light for protection.

3. Play your music, set your timer, light your candle and allow yourself to focus on your breath, or the candle or the music and just see where it will take you.

4. When the timer goes off, give yourself this time to journal any thoughts that came to you. Experiment this week with the different **tools**. What did you like? What did you not like? Which **tool** had the best results this week?

5. Do your centering breath work along with the candle flame exercise daily, either in the morning, evening or during the day. This should take you no more than 5 minutes. If you come out of your meditation and find you spent more than 5 minutes and you are pleasantly surprised, note it in your journal along with any insight that you received during meditation.

6. Remember to finish each meditating session with gratitude. So…when the timer goes off just say out loud, "I give thanks".

7. Journal after you meditate. I recommend it while you are learning to meditate because you are opening yourself up to receiving guidance from your intuition and the energy of all that is and connects us all. I also recommend that you get yourself a small pocket

size notebook to keep on you because now that you are tuning into your intuition, you will get the answers to questions you have been pondering. By answers I mean, a word may pop into your consciousness, or you may see a solution to something you have been trying to work out. These things don't always happen when you are meditating! They happen while you are driving, or in the shower or even grocery shopping! When the mind and the heart are in unison, working in harmony, profound wisdom is tapped into and depending on your own wiring, you get those messages when you are ready.

8. Practice the sun salutation every day. Try doing it in the morning some days, and in the evening other days.

So.....how do you feel? There is a lot of new thought here to open your mind to a new way of thinking and learning. This information may feel a little strange at first to grasp, but please remember...you are the one that wanted to learn a new way of being, so no judgments on what is said....just allow the information to flow into you and see what tools work for you.

Have an amazing week ☺

A NOTE FROM THE UNIVERSE

Starting something is the best way to finish something. And just doing a teeny, tiny something today, anything, from wherever you are, is the best way to start something.

I'm not just a client,

The Universe

Today. Make a call, ask a question, search the web, buy a book, pound the pavement, measure, cut, paste, poke, and of course, give thanks in advance.

If you would like to receive your own daily notes from the Universe, please visit www.tut.com and sign up.

Week 2:

OBJECTIVES OF MEDITATION

Where there is peace and meditation,
there is neither anxiety nor doubt.
~St. Francis de Sales

So? How did last week go? *Write your response here:*

Meditation was challenging - difficulty focusing
but kept at it

_____

_____

What is something positive that happened this past week for you? *Write your response below:*

Financial Policy – hard work payed

off

_____

_____

_____

This week we are going to talk about the objectives of meditation, the origins of meditation, the ego and healing with meditation.

THE THREE OBJECTIVES OF MEDITATION

1. Preliminary: To improve your bodily health and mental stability, meaning to reduce the stress level on your body.

2. Intermediate: To continue to increase, harmonize and integrate your thoughts, emotions, desires, aims, motives and reasoning. By doing so, you will be more objective of yourself and how you react to situations, so you are in harmony. (Mind)

3. Finally: Liberation! – This means having awareness of access to your psychic and mental ability to attain the state of self-realization. (Spirit). To acquire this skill, you will need to change a few things.

   a) Purification of the body- eating foods that are nutritional for us. Stay away from processed foods. Eat fresh fruits and veggies, drink lots of water, if you choose to eat meat, buy local from a farm that harvests sustainably and reverently. Make sure your fruits and veggies are grown without pesticides or GMO's. A great way to do this is to grow your own food. If you had to make your own sweets instead of buying pre-made and pre-wrapped, you would eat less of them. When eating out,know what you are eating. If you aren't sure, you can always bring your own food to whatever event you are attending.

   b) Removal of impurities in your thoughts - thinking, feeling, doing should all be the same. Release external distractions. You do this when you center yourself, breath with intention, and choose to meditate. You can make the choice to stop participating in the gossip at work or lose your cool when someone cuts you off in traffic. Choose to turn off the television, news and limit the time you spend in front of you smart devices e.g. phone, laptop, tablets etc. Anytime you tap into fear, sadness or anger, you lower your vibration. A very simple, easy and effective way to raise your vibration is through gratitude. When you feel that your vibration is low, stop, think and clear and then think of something you are grateful for.

c) Consciousness being clear and pure – allowing one to see how they are connected to all that is. Immerse yourself in this new feeling of learning that everything and everyone is connected. That everything is made up of energy. When you think about yourself, see yourself as part of the entire Earth picture. I like to do this by hugging a tree or sitting under the stars at night. My very favorite way to raise my own vibration is to surround myself with like-minded people who share the same path I am on. I am very fortunate to have found an amazing group of people who share and believe in the same ideals and principles. I am truly blessed.

When I get into that "stinkin thinkin" I stop, clear and reach out to one of those people in my tribe (as I like to call them) and seek their knowledge. For that...I am truly humbled.

Einstein once said: *"Imagination is more important than knowledge." Thus, allow your own imagination to show you the possibilities of who and how you are meant to be."*

The use of meditation has been around for thousands of years. Meditation techniques have always been a part of an attempt to alter the natural human condition, with its physical pain, always changing and unstable emotions and its ego centered thinking.

Over five thousand years ago, the ancient Egyptians meditated, evidenced by the depictions and pictures that were left on the walls of tombs showing yogis in meditation. The I-Ching book was being created in China over four thousand years ago and we still benefit from its insights today.

The great prophets of The Old Testament lived over 3,500 years ago, yet we still gather to listen and study those teachings and meditation is mentioned in the Old Testament.

We also have the sacred books called The Vedas which were being written about this same time in India. I have a wonderful reference to where people have found the 'gifts of the spirit' in the bible. You can get it at my website. *All of these insights came when people were in a higher consciousness during meditation, and they were first uttered by sages, saints, seers and shamans who became spiritual giants as a result of lives shaped by meditation. Your spirituality has nothing to do with what you believe, it has everything to do with your state of consciousness.*

Now I would like to talk about what I have referred to as the "ego". I like to refer to the ego as that child that needs attention. I've taken enough psychology classes to understand the ego from that type of perspective, however I want to share with you my views of the ego from an "authentic self" perspective. This is the perception I have personally gained from the classes I have taken in traditional accredited schools in addition to the classes, workshops and books which were not available in academia at the time I was educating myself in this arena.

The ego attaches to things as self-identification thinking enhancement. I, ME, MINE are attachment words.

The ego is part of the unconscious self that likes to let you know when to be afraid, tell you what to do and voices all the negativity and possibly some positivity, because, you know….you can't be too positive about yourself, said NO ONE EVER!!!! When you are experiencing the feeling of anxiety, anger or anything upsetting, you are attached to the thought. Thought forms are that which the ego can identify with. For example, if you don't want to go somewhere and you use the excuse "I am sick" when really, you are healthy and are simply choosing not to go, if you keep using the excuse "I am sick", before you know it, you will be sick!

When we incorporate meditation into our daily practices, we will begin to heal ourselves. Healing with meditation deals with 'mind stuff' and bringing the body, energy and mind into harmony with each other by changing what the mind's eye perceives. Meditation is a state of mind, and includes a point of view about the world, ourselves, and how we interact in that world.

Meditation helps us to become more conscious of our own body and aids us in listening with respect to what it is telling us. This helps us to recognize and then minimize whatever is causing physical disharmony and stress, which is an important aspect of healing. We are asked to listen, to look and accept what is there without censorship or judgement. Acceptance is also an important part of healing.

This means that you learn to surrender and accept your whole self. Surrendering is not giving up, it is acceptance of what is. Enlightenment, Liberation, Surrender, are all words to describe your awakening to your authentic self and your transformation.

There are 3 concepts of meditation. They are:

1. Mindfulness – to calm the mind and the 5 senses.

2. Concentration – concentration is developed through trance. This contains an assumption that consciousness includes two separate levels: a surface mind and an inner mind. The surface mind is continually disrupted, the inner mind in eternally calm and quiet.

3. Wisdom – which is achieved when you have returned from a meditative state of the inner mind, where your consciousness is altered and you begin to see things more clearly.

A monk by the name of Thich Nhat Hanh wrote a book about being mindful in your daily life. I saw him speak once at Dartmouth. I had three very small children at the time and man, could I use some mindfulness. I was so preoccupied with doing so much and being so tired all the time that when I saw this Tibetan monk, he brought me to tears.

He spoke about being mindful when you are doing the dishes. Being thankful for the food you have to feed your family. Being thankful for the running warm water to wash the dishes. Being mindful for the dishes and the soap to clean them. He was one of those influences in my life that had a big impact on me. I bought his book and have shared it with so many people over the years. When he spoke of that, I thought he was speaking to me. That's how I felt...like all I did was do everything for everyone else. I was frustrated because isn't this what I wanted, this family? Then why am I so agitated because all I do is care for them? By Thich teaching me to be mindful, I became less agitated and more grateful and it has become a part of who I am today. I go through my day constantly being grateful for small things and I am a happier being!

Here is a wonderful poem I love, and speaks about what we are all feeling as we embark on our journeys.

When you wake up to the true meaning of why you are here,

Something happens as you align with the Divine.

As you become one with it, really ONE,

you start to feel it, somewhere deep inside

a feeling that cannot be told or explained, it is simply a knowing

that your life is beautiful

perfect and is unfolding exactly, in the most flawless way it should.

You understand that you are in the flow

that this is working at the exact speed and timing that is perfect for you and you begin to simply JUST BE and trust the process.

You begin to really enjoy each moment in your life.

You realize that you have been taught something different from birth.

The beliefs of life is hard or things are limited..... And somewhere inside, within your cells you know you must let these go...these limiting thoughts don't fit you anymore because you know different.

You don't do this in a way that you are giving up on your dreams, instead you relax into this new thought of life's beautiful creation coming together almost like a symphony around you.

This returns you to a childlike wonder, to see where this flow will take you next. You are excited to see your life unfold around you like you are looking into a snow globe. As you remain detached, you are also captivated by how it will all appear as the story of your life.

And you step back, allowing, trusting, that no matter what, whatever happens will be your dream life, in a way that cannot ever be foretold.

You feel that deep knowing inside, as a co-creator with the Source of your life, you don't need to have a plan, you don't need to cling to what you believe you need, but instead allow it to come to you.

You JUST BE, living in happy peace, watching the cycles of life with wonder at its spectacular beauty. You relax knowing that what action or step you need to do next will come to you at the perfect time

If you encounter delays or problems, you welcome them in, trusting that they are flawless for the unfolding of your dream.

You JUST BE as you begin to co-create your life in front of your eyes.

"He who controls others may be powerful... but he who has mastered himself is mightier still." - Lao Tzu

PRACTICE EXERCISE FOR WEEK TWO

This week, I want you to be aware of what little insights you are getting. Write down things that are all of a sudden crossing your path such as: maybe you are in need of someone to help with something and you thought about it in your meditation and asked for help and voila! Now it has crossed your path! Write that stuff down! Or if you get a message and aren't sure the meaning... write it down so you can go back and look at it later.

Use these tips to get the most out of your meditation:

1. Be comfortable. Let your whole body sink downward, imagine it is being attracted by the force of gravity. Let your spine sink towards the surface you are on, especially at the waist level. When lying on a flat surface, it helps to raise your knees, with your feet about shoulder width apart and your toes pointing up to keep your knees from falling inward, possibly placing a rolled up towel under the back of your knees. If you sit in a reclining position, let your spine sink into the chair. If you sit upright, keep your spine vertical so you aren't putting any strain on your back muscles. Just stay relaxed, keep your chin slightly tucked in, your neck long and drop your shoulders.

2. Relax your face, gently smile to yourself to get your face to relax.

3. Breathe from your diaphragm, so your abdomen rises as you breathe in and sinks back as you exhale. Do not hold in your belly.

4. Be in a room with soft lighting. A shaded lamp is better than a ceiling light and both are better than a fluorescent light.

5. Set time aside for meditation so you will not have any disturbances from the phone, family or visitors.

6. Keeping your eyes gently closed will assist you to focus within. Remove your glasses if you wear them.

7. You may become more relaxed than you are used to, if you are uncomfortable, reposition yourself. To relax your body, tighten different areas, then release. Start from the feet and move up to your head.

8. If thoughts go through your mind, it is all right. Let your thoughts come in on the right side of your brain, acknowledge them, and release them out through the left side of the brain. Tell yourself you are doing this correctly. Only by continued practice will it become natural and easy for you.

9. You may feel unusual sensations such as floating or tingling. Enjoy them and recognize that they reflect positive inner changes in you.

10. Many people find it easier to meditate in the morning when their mind is still calm, or at the end of the day when there are no demands on you.

Remember to journal so you may record any experiences you have, memories or ideas.

Use these two handouts. Feel free to make a copy and cut them out to stick where you will see them twice a day. Put one on your bathroom mirror so you read it when you brush your teeth in the morning and when you brush your teeth at night before going to bed. ☺

OPENING GREETING

As I open myself to the Unseen Forces which

surround The Throne of Grace, Mercy and Light,

I surround myself with the pure white light of Protection

found in the thoughts of the Divine.

Only Thy will be done in and through me.

POSITIVE AFFIRMATION

There are no circumstances beyond my control.

All I have is given to me by my Higher Self because I am
ready to meet, handle and embrace it.

All is for my benefit and spiritual awakening.

I accept all from the

Source of Love and Acceptance.

I am, have been, and forever will be a co-creator with the
Divine.

I release all that hinders me and accept the divine will of my authentic self.

TO DO THIS WEEK:

1. Continue to fine tune your meditation practice. You've had a week to use the tools from week one and I have introduced you to some other points this week. Choose what is working for you and note it. Do you have certain music you like? A favorite candle? How about a favorite pen to write in you journal? Any small adjustments that you can make will only further enhance your meditative practice.

A NOTE FROM THE UNIVERSE

The path to enlightenment is not a path at all, it's actually a metaphor for the time it takes for you to allow yourself to be happy with who you already are, where you're already at, and what you already have – no matter what.

If you would like to receive your own daily notes from the Universe, please visit <u>www.tut.com</u> and sign up.

Week 3:

A DEEPER LOOK AT MEDITATION

How did last week go? *Write your response below now*:

_____

_____

_____

_____

_____

_____

What is something positive that happened this past week for you? *Write your response in the journal now*:

_____

_____

_____

_____

_____

_____

This week we are going to take a deeper look at Meditation. We will discuss the brain division, do an overview of the Chakra system (because that *alone* could be its own book!), the auric field, the meridian system and discuss taking the 3 practical steps towards meditation.

To help you understand how this process, let me explain a little about how your brain works. You have 2 sides to your brain:

1. Left Side: which is most commonly used to think logically, do mathematics, reason deductively, remember details, and measure time.

This governs the **right** side of the body, and is generally concerned with logical thinking, speech and practical matters. For many, the right hand, foot and eye are the dominant ones. Yogis consider this energy to be dynamic or vital.

2. Right Side: is your intuitive thinking, imagination, memory, psychic abilities and instant understanding.

This side governs the *left* side of the body, and is concerned with space, creativity and intuition. It sees things all as one piece rather than sequentially, and is good at lateral thinking – the unexpected sideways jump by which new discoveries are made. Yogis consider this energy as mental.

When you use both sides together, you access your *higher abstract mind.*

For more great information about the brain, check out Mark Waldman who is one of the world's leading experts on communication, spirituality, and the brain. He is on the faculty at Loyola Marymount University's College of Business and the Holmes Institute. For more information, I suggest you check out his website and read about his 10 mind blowing discoveries about the human brain at www.markrobertwaldman.com.

This week, I want to introduce you to another breathing technique called 'alternate nostril breathing.' This is used to achieve balance between inwardness and outwardness, and to balance the brain.

The thumb is used to close off the right nostril, the two middle fingers rest against the forehead, and the ring and little finger are used to close off the left nostril. The left hand rests in your lap. Let's try it:

Breath out, now close your right nostril, breathe in through the left, Close the left nostril and open the right nostril, now breathe out through it. Now breathe in through the right nostril, close off the right nostril and open the left nostril and exhale. Repeat. Do this several times and then check in with yourself. How do you feel?

We have this beautiful body that is affected by the moons cycles (yes, men and women!), the sun's cycles and the earth's magnetic field. We are constantly pulling people and experiences into our lives that are a match to your own magnetic field or vibration, according to quantum physics.

Your human body has different elements in it such as salt, magnesium, copper and iron just to name a few. Why are we so astounded, or even hard headed to believe we are affected by the moon and sun (such as SAD seasonal affected disorder) along with certain rocks or crystals from the earth? People from all cultures travel to certain areas to sit in the salt sea or hot springs or even caves with certain crystals in them which are known for their healing properties.

The molecular structure of your cells are vibrating at different frequencies to keep them together. Your vibration can go higher or lower depending on the emotion you are experiencing. A happy emotion tends to have a faster and higher vibratory frequency, while a sad emotion will have a slower and lower vibratory frequency. To learn more about this great work, check out the Emotional Scale Spiral by Esther and Jerry Hicks.

So, if meditation is the transforming of one's mind to acquire peace and tranquility, and meditation means awareness, and awareness means the ability to perceive, feel or be conscious of events, objects, thoughts, emotions or sensory patterns, doesn't it then make sense that we need vibrational elements to assist us in collecting and interpreting all this information so we can receive healing?

Have you ever been taught about the human energy fields? I will touch on them briefly here, because, again...this is a whole other book!! Some schools of thought believe we have 7 major ones inside our body and many minor ones known as chakras. We have another system known as meridians and there is the Auric system that is the energy field outside and around your human body.

The Auric system is a field of energy which surrounds and penetrates the body to communicate with the chakra system and the meridian system. The aura underlies and supports the functioning of the body. Within the aura there are 7 levels. They are the energetic aspects of every structure and function of the body, as well as everything that we experience (physical, thoughts, feelings, states of consciousness, etc.) Some people are able to see the auric field. If you cannot see the auric field around others or yourself, you can experience it through Kirlian photography, where someone will take a photograph of you and it will show your auric field! I have had it personally done three times. Each time my auric photo has been different in color and shape and this gives me powerful insight into what is going on with the outer frequency of my body, and how it is manifesting in my physical body. For example, imagine you are in the kitchen doing the dishes, someone tries to sneak up on you and just before they get to you, you turn around....that's because you *had a feeling* and acted on it. You turned and caught them before they could get to you. That was your auric field letting you know someone was in your personal space.

The Chakra system. The word chakra means wheel. The chakra system has 3 main functions: 1. To energize the body, 2. To bring about the awareness of self-development and 3. To transmit spiritual energy. We have 7 major chakras in our body and many minor chakras throughout the beautiful vessel of our human body. Below is a graph of the chakras and important information. Each major chakra is numbered 1 through 7, we begin with the lower 1st chakra found at the base of our spine, our root chakra. Please refer to the graph on the following page for all the important information of what color is associated with the chakra, and where it is located in the body along with more information on what part of the body is affected by that particular chakra.

In Hinduism, a chakra is thought to be an energy

node in the human body. Chakra is a Sanskrit word meaning wheel, or vortex. It refers to each of the seven energy centers that our consciousness and energy systems are composed.

These chakras or energy centers function as pumps or valves, regulating the flow of energy through our energy system.

The functioning of the chakras reflects decisions we make concerning how we choose to respond to condition in our lives.

As with all things in our reality, the chakras are linked to sound, light and color. The base chakra (red) is where the Kundalini energy also known as the sleeping serpent is located. It lies dormant in most people unless it is activated. It is a very powerful energy that shoots up through the entire body activating all the chakras as it passes through them and out the top of the head.

Each major chakra is also associated with a glandular system of your body. Dr. Carolyn Myss does an amazing job giving in depth details on the chakras and the organs associated with them along with information on the mental, emotional and physical issues and dysfunctions that can be within each chakra. I recommend her book *Anatomy of the Spirit* for this information.

The Hindu study of the chakra system brings in more elements that we are affected by. Each chakra is associated with a main principle, mantra sound, musical note, metal, planet, crystal and aroma. There are essential oils now that are recommended for the various chakras. Each energy center or chakra has a female or male rotation to it and spins either clockwise or counter-clockwise. Each chakra has harmonious attributes and disharmonious attributes.

The meridian system is an 'energy highway' if you will, in the human body. Ki or Qi or Prana energy flows through this system accessing all parts of the body.

Meridians of the body affect every organ and physiological system inside of us. They are invisible to the human eye, yet without them we could not sustain life. In the same way that arteries carry blood, meridians carry energy.

These pathways bring vitality and balance, remove energy blockages, stagnations and imbalances, adjust metabolism and determine the speed and form of cellular change. They affect all major systems including: immune, nervous, endocrine, circulatory, respiratory, digestive, skeletal, muscular and the lymphatic system. If a meridian's energy is obstructed or unregulated, the system it feeds on is jeopardized, and the possibility of disease could be a result.

All this information is important if you are to understand and make the connection on how imperative it is to first know yourself, and the best way to do that is through meditation.

There are three practical steps or fundamental attitudes for meditation and they are:

1. **Self-Discipline** – this makes us regular at practicing what it is we wish to master, i.e. Meditation.

2. **Self-Knowledge** – most of us have only a vague idea of what goes on in our bodies and our minds. Yet, universal laws operate within us, like everything else. This new awareness brings new responsibility. We can no longer blame others for everything unpleasant that happens to us. Changing our world, starts with ourselves.

3. **Self- Surrender** – this is an affair of the heart, letting go of your ego centeredness, such as: do we want to sleep late, or do we want to honor and keep up our regular practice of meditation? ☺

I want to share with you that I am an energy medicine practitioner. I have been trained in a modality called Reiki and I love doing reiki on others and myself. I would like to share an inspirational saying, the Reiki Ideals with you:

"May today there be peace within you, May you trust your highest self that you are exactly where you are

meant to be, May you not forget the infinite possibilities that are born of faith, May you use those gifts that you have received and pass on the love that has been given to you, May you be content knowing you are a child of this universe, Let this presence settle into your bones and allow your soul the freedom to sing, dance and to bask in the eternal sun. It is there for each and every one of you."

PRACTICE EXERCISE FOR WEEK THREE

For This week's meditation practice, I am going to give you my **signature chakra clearing exercise.** **Read through this once, then keep it nearby so you can refer to it at any time.**

1. Sit in a chair with your feet on the ground. Do your three cleansing breaths. With your eyes closed, see yourself surrounded by radiant white light engulfing you like an egg shell.

2. Picture that light now penetrating through your skin so you can feel it throughout your body in your veins. Feel it move through your entire body, surrounding your organs and traveling in your bloodstream.

3. Now see it with your mind's eye coming out of the bottom of your feet and reaching down towards the Earth, going through the floor, moving rock and dirt, searching for the energy source at the center of our Earth. Once you find it, attach yourself to it and bring that energy light up through the rock and dirt, through the floor, enter the bottom of your feet and slowly travel up past your toes, heels, ankles, shins, calves, knees, thighs, hips, and the base of your spine.

4. See this light travel up your spine into your head and exit out of the top of your head, shooting up through the ceiling, through the roof. Go up into the sky, past the trees and the stars, and out into our galaxy, past the Milky Way, searching for that universal stream of consciousness that is out there.

5. When you find it, tap into it and bring that energy back down through the galaxy, past the stars into the sky, past the trees into your roof and the ceiling and enter into the top or your head. As it does, feel it gently cascade down the front of your body like warm water and connect into the earth, then have it come back up the backside of your body and out of the top of your head into the universe and know now that you are connected above and below.

6. Now I want you to take this beautiful white light and see it at the base of your spine in the 1st chakra, the root chakra. Here is where we hold onto things that have happened in our past. To release this, I want you to repeat after me, "**I release my past to the universe**"

7. Bring the light up to the 2nd chakra, the reproductive area where we hold onto worries of what is to come. Release this by repeating after me, "**I release my future to the universe**"

8. Continue the light up to the 3rd chakra, the solar plexus, where we hold onto fears. Fear is nothing but lack of knowledge and is wasted energy so let's clear that out by having you repeat after me, "**I release my fear to the universe**"

9. Now bring the light up into your heart, feel it warm your chest area and your heart and lungs. Here we just want to re-affirm, "**The universe is love**"

10. Bring it up into your throat chakra, this is the vibration you put out into the world with your words. Let's be more mindful of what we say by repeating after me, "**The universe is peace**"

11. And bring it up further past your chin, lips and nose and allow it to settle between your two eyebrows above the bridge of your nose and feel this 3rd eye chakra opening and just repeat after me, "**The universe is Spirit**"

12. Take that beautiful white light up to the top of your head and just reaffirm, "**The universe is All**".

Now sit with this energy and calmness for as long as you wish. Remember to give thanks at the end of your meditation by saying, "**I give thanks**"

TO DO THIS WEEK:

1. Practice the alternate nostril breathing technique at least three times this week to see how you like or dislike it. It's important when doing something new to do it for a minimum of three times to really see if you like it, or not.

2. I want you to do the above guided meditation of grounding and clearing out your chakras. Play your favorite music softly in the background. Have a candle lit or use a battery operated candle.

3. Meditate at different times of the day. Do it one day in the morning and then another day in the evening. How was it different? Note it in your journal. Also note any other insights or awareness that have come to your consciousness.

A Note from the Universe

No, you probably can't see it yet, but I can. Wheels are now turning that have never turned before. Winds are now howling that have never howled before. And players from every walk of life are being drawn into place as if in some hypnotic dance. All because of you, your dreams, and your divinely stubborn persistence.

If I wasn't the Universe, I don't think I'd believe it.
Phew-w-w-w-w-w...
The Universe

Week 4:

THE DIFFERENT TYPES OF MEDITATION

How did last week go? *Write your response below:*

_____

_____

_____

_____

_____

_____

What is something positive that happened this past week for you? *Write your response below:*

_____

_____

_____

_____

_____

_____

"Watch your thoughts, they become your words;

Watch your words, they become your actions;

Watch your actions, they become your habits;

Watch your habits, they become your character;

Watch your character, it becomes your destiny."

- Lao Tzu

I love that quote from Lao Tzu because it keeps me in the present moment.

This week I am going to introduce you to a few meditation modalities you may not have heard of, or maybe you have but you haven't experienced before. I want to briefly explain Eastern Mantras and Christian Meditation. I also want to share with you the importance of group meditation, using visualization and touch on channeling. Let's get started.

MANTRA MEANS:
THOUGHT FORM *OR* MIND POWER.

The first purpose of a mantra is to draw your mind away from the trivial and the superficial, drawing your thoughts away from worldly things, such as fear, concerns or apprehensions.

The second purpose of using a mantra is it sets up a rhythm, and that rhythm controls your prana (energy), changing your breathing pattern ever so slightly.

The third purpose of a mantra is the words in the mantra are symbols which have cultural and universal meaning to your personal unconscious as well as the collective unconscious.

In meditation, we are working to get away from the superficial, surface living, and to gain an order in the subconscious mind to induce positive feelings, creative states, and the balancing of any unconscious negative karma, permanently. Whether we realize it or not, we seek meditation to get specific answers about life.

There is a wonderful example of this on YouTube called 'Mantra de los 7 chakras', and I encourage you to listen to it and experience it. It's a beautiful rhythmical example of an Eastern Mantra.

Let's talk about Christian Meditative techniques.

We have Prayer: the recognition that you need help in order to change your life. *Divine Intervention*. Prayer is asking for assistance with something in your life. The goal of meditative prayer is to help and comfort others through the use of your own mind power. The development of compassion will bring spiritual unfoldment. The important take away here is you can send healing vibrations to another person. When you do this, it's important to ask for the 'highest and best for the situation' because everyone has free will.

Then we have Affirmations: an affirmation is pulling yourself together, and helping yourself by replacing a negative outlook with a positive outlook. Affirmations are sentences or phrases which state in the present tense, those qualities we do not now have, but hope to acquire in the near future. It can be observed from these descriptions, that both prayer and affirmations involve us in recognizing something is amiss, and then doing something about it.

We also have Mantras; which start changes in us without any need for us first to consider what may be wrong in our personal circumstances or attitudes. By sitting quietly, letting go of all anxiety and settling the mind and repeating the mantra, we allow something to happen WITHIN US. Mantra practice raises our vibrations, so we are more in touch with the divine within, more capable of seeing things differently, and are able to change our attitudes accordingly.

In the United States and other parts of the modern world, the pressure to always be actively busy is making our nervous systems very unbalanced. We need to incorporate regular periods during our day where we stop 'doing' and start 'being'. In making this shift, we will learn to be more present and focus on the NOW.

Throughout history, Christianity has always had groups of people who were encouraged to keep this balance by living in seclusion in monasteries and convents. Their days are lived in a rhythm where activity alternates between periods of silence, chanting, private prayer and meditation.

Wherever there is praise *to* God, rather than a request *for* something, there lies a mantra.

An example of this is The Lord's Prayer. It starts and ends with a string of mantras where the focus is always on God, thereby lifting us up and out of ourselves.

Another example would be the Taize Experience. This is when a word is set to music and the word or phrase is chanted/sung over and over again. The tune is set in 4 parts, such as the Alleluia!

GROUP MEDITATION

What I like about teaching Meditation & Awareness, either in person or in a virtual classroom, is that my students not only learn how to set up their own space for meditation but they also get the benefits of the support from one another in a group led meditation that I finish each class session with.

Group meditation is one of my favorite experiences I have ever had. When you meditate in a group there are mirror neurons in your brain that make the experience not 10 times or 15 times more powerful, it is more powerful to the 10th or 15th degree. And not just for you, but for everyone in the group! Group meditation can also recharge your dedication to your meditation practice. You will feel refreshed and balanced from the experience, which will lead you to want to continue meditating on your own.

As you meditate and your consciousness expands, you will then be thirsty for more knowledge regarding the unfoldment of your awareness, and your intellect will begin to look at things in your life that you believe no longer serve you.

Some group meditations I have attended will have a shared intention such as for Healing or World Peace. Group meditation will help you to strengthen your own practice, support one another, and it will assist those who are new to meditating by learning more from the experienced meditators in the group. It's important to always end each meditation practice whether in a group or alone, with giving thanks. This can be done simply by saying 'we give thanks' collectively to close the group meditation.

VISUALIZATION

Visualization is another great empowering **tool** I use in my classroom settings. I like to give a sample of all the different techniques such that are used in meditation so my students are continually stimulated. This really encourages the student to continue with their daily meditation practice. Visualization is a great **tool** way of promoting the body, mind and spirit connection and to expand your self-awareness.

Using visualization has been cited to have numerous health benefits such as; decreasing stress, alleviating chronic pain or headaches, easing depression, relieving insomnia and more importantly…boosting your immune system. *Holistic Online* is a great resource that cites studies from many universities which prove the benefits.

The act of 'seeing yourself' in your mind's eye as completely healthy or accomplishing a goal is as good as the action itself. Studies on our human brain now show our thoughts produce the same mental instructions as our actions. The results highlight the strength between the mind-body connections, in essence your thoughts-behaviors, are very important for achieving your best life.

The electrical impulses of neurons in our brains transmit information by interpreting images as equal to performing the action. Essentially, our brains don't understand the difference between imagined, and what we actually do in our daily lives.

When we use visualization, the Brain's neurons interpret the thought as a movement. This creates a new neural pathway, a cluster of cells in our brain which works together and create an imprint of the visualized behavior. This makes the mind-body connection interpret the visualization as IF the physical motion was already completed.

A study observing brain patterns discovered that the patterns activated when a person performed the activity, were also activated when they only imagined they were performing the activity. In some cases, research has shown that mental practices are almost as effective as true physical practice, and that doing both would give the optimum results.
(http://www.ncbi.nlm.nih.gov/pubmed/14998709).

If we were to develop a daily practice of visualization, it would strengthen our communication between the mind and the body giving us the opportunity to achieve our very best outcome.

When you use a visualization it's important to start off in a positive mind set. Don't try to do this if you are angry, upset or agitated. Work on getting yourself in a relaxed state of consciousness. You can do this by using your breath, centering yourself and connecting yourself above and below.

Next you want to bring into your relaxed state of consciousness the thought of what it is you desire. Imagine all the details; what are the physical senses you can attach to the desire? For example, the sights, smells, tastes, what you hear and more importantly, *how does it feel*?

Once this is complete, and your emotion is attached to your desire, it's time to see its completion in your mind's eye. After you come out of your visualization, think about a step you can actually do now to move closer to creating what you want.

It's important to do this so the universal vibration knows you are actively working with it to co-create what it is you want. So, if your desire is to get a new job, then in your visualization you want to see yourself at your new job, the location, and the sounds around the office, the smells and how it *feels* to be there. After you have done all of this (it shouldn't take more than a few minutes), you may want to take action by doing a search on the internet for jobs, or update your resume.

CHANNELING

Channeling refers to the ability of communicating with spirit guides or a consciousness that is not in a human body form. That consciousness is expressed through the channel or channeler.

A channeler is someone who can connect with and receive information from a higher spiritual realm. We talked about how we have seven levels as part of our human energetic field, or also referred to as 7 planes of consciousness. The common form of communication with the nonphysical consciousness is with people who have passed on, and a person who can communicate with this consciousness is known as a medium.

The commonality of a medium and channeler is they can access higher knowledge for the benefit of spiritual growth and clarity in one's life. Have you ever been to a medium? Have you attended an event to see someone who can channel? I have experienced both and they are very enlightening.

We live in a multidimensional universe, so doesn't it make sense that we are able to connect with other energetic forms, when we are vibrating at a high frequency so we are then able to communicate? An example that comes to mind for me is how a dog can hear frequencies that are not detectable to the human ear. Dogs are able to hear a higher frequency we humans cannot detect.

PRACTICE EXERCISE FOR WEEK FOUR

Now that you have all these ***tools*** and exercises, continue to use them and get familiar with what is resonating with you *now* to use. All references to practices in this book are also available on my website for you to use. I hope you have enjoyed this introduction to Meditation & Awareness. I invite you to continue to develop your meditation practice and as your quest for spiritual knowledge continues to unfold, you continue to search for answers.

Once you have worked through this material, I invite you to explore the deeper meanings of some of the topics I touched on here, in my next book which will take on a journey to a passage of a higher consciousness, where we will go deeper into the Chakra System, Vibrational Medicine, the 7 Energetic Fields and Channeling just to name a few!

Check out my website for future on-line group sessions that you may want to join.

TO DO THIS WEEK:

1. Take the time this week to listen to the Mantras on YouTube called 'Mantra de los 7 chakras'. Before you begin to listen to it, ground yourself and clear out your chakras like I have taught you in the previous chapters.

2. Listen to the guided visualization I have offered to you. You can find it at www.debbiesodergren.com and download it for your personal use.

3. In the coming months, invest in yourself by seeking out a group meditation to participate in locally. If you are interested, you may even seek out the online group meditation I host.

A NOTE FROM THE UNIVERSE

Do you know why we, in the unseen, love Fridays every
bit as much as you?
Because on Fridays, all of the angels regroup and share stories
of the remarkable heroism, incredible beauty, and heartfelt
love witnessed all over your astounding little planet.

Thanks for being part of it all,
The Universe

RECOMMENDED READING

The following books have had an incredible impact on my life. You will absolutely love them.

Infinite Possibilities by Mike Dooley

Frank Talk by Tracy Farquhar

Do You Quantum Think? By Dianne Collins

Energy Medicine by Dr. Norm Shealy

Anatomy Of The Spirit by Caroline Myss

The Spiritual Universe by Fred Alan Wolf, PhD

Auras by Edgar Cayce

Heal Your Body by Louise Hay

Hands of Light by Barbara Ann Brennan

Wheels of Light by Rosalyn L. Bruyere

Kundalini and the Chakras by Genevieve Lewis Paulson

Healing with Chakra Energy by Lilla Bek

The Healer's Manual by Ted Andrews

Vibrational Medicine by Dr. Richard Gerber

A Guide to Spirit Healing by Harry Edwards

Edgar Cayce Book of Drugless Therapy by Dr. Harold Reilly

Scientific Healing Affirmations by P. Yogananda

Ageless Body Timeless Mind by Depok Chopra

The Indigo Children by Lee Carroll & Jan Tober

The Case for Reincarnation by Joe Fisher

I recommend you look into the following Publications to discover more about meditation and awareness.

Natural Awakenings

Modern Meditation

The Door Opener

Body + Soul

The Quest

Mindful Magazine

Yoga Journal

New Age Magazine

ABOUT THE AUTHOR

Debbie Sodergren is an Energy Medicine Practitioner, Public Speaker and Mentor. Debbie graduated from the New England School of Metaphysical Studies in 1998. She is nationally certified as a Reiki Master Teacher, is certified to teach Metaphysics and Meditation and is an Infinite Possibilities Trailblazer.

Debbie has a deep understanding of the body, mind and spirit connection. Her philosophy of healing is based on the client being taken care of with traditional allopathic medicine along with alternative healing modalities to ensure that the individual's whole self is being maintained and balanced.

To this end, Debbie has trained extensively in the human energy field in areas of chakra balancing, vibrational medicine, channeling, death and dying, meditation, infinite possibilities mindset, and more.

Made in the
USA
Middletown, DE

74521599R10049